UNCOVERING THE PAST:
ANALYZING PRIMARY SOURCES

THE WAR
OF 1812

THE STAR SPANGLED BANNER.

SIMON ADAMS

CRABTREE
PUBLISHING COMPANY
WWW.CRABTREEBOOKS.COM

Author: Simon Adams

Editor-in-Chief: Lionel Bender

Editors: Simon Adams, Ellen Rodger

Proofreaders: Laura Booth, Angela Kaelberer

Project coordinator: Petrice Custance

Design and photo research: Ben White

Production: Kim Richardson

**Production coordinator and
   prepress technician:** Ken Wright

Print coordinator: Katherine Berti

Consultant: Emily Drew
   The New York Public Library

Produced for Crabtree Publishing Company
by Bender Richardson White

Photographs and reproductions:
Alamy: 4–5, 29 Btm (North Wind Picture Archives), 7 (INTERFOTO), 10 (Library of Congress/S.Dupuis), 26 (Paul Fearn); Library of Congress: Top Left (Icon) 4, 6 (LC-USZC4-6893), 8–9 (LOC pnp/ppmsca.10756), 11 (LC-DIG-ppmsc-05876), 13 Left (LC-H824-T01-0523), 13 Right (LC-DIG-ppmsca-31279), 14 (LC-USZC4-6222), 15 Top (LC-DIG-pga-10152), 15 Btm (LC-USZ62-5338), Top Left (Icon) 16, 18 (LC-DIG-pga-09625), 19 (LC-DIG-ppmsca-10754), Top Left (Icon) 20, 22, 24, 26, 28, 30, 32 (LC-DIG-pga-01838), 20–21 (LC-DIG-pga-02159), 24 (LC-DIG-hec-25920), 28 (LC-DIG-pga-05783), 29 Top (LC-DIG-ppmsca-31112), 30 Top (LC-USZ62-132786), 30 Btm (LC-DIG-pga-01011), 31 (LC-DIG-pga-01838), Top Left (Icon) 34, 36 (LC-DIG-ppmsca-09855), 37 (LC-DIG-pga-08576); Library and Archives Canada: 40, 41 top; Shutterstock: 6 (J.T. Lewis), Top Left (Icon) 8, 10, 12, 14 (J.T. Lewis), 36 Top (Rook76), 36 Btm (SF photo), 41 Btm (Sergei Bachlakov); Topfoto: 12, 16–17, 18, 22–23, 23, 25, 32, 34–35, 35 (The Granger Collection), 27 (World History Archive); Wikimedia.org: front cover (John David Kelly), 38 Btm Right, 40 (United States public domain
Photo courtesy of the Chatham Voice: 39 Btm Right
Photo courtesy of Mike Kubes: 39, 39 Top

Map: Stefan Chabluk

Cover: Image of the death of General Brock at the Battle of Queenston Heights

---

Library and Archives Canada Cataloguing in Publication

Adams, Simon, 1955-, author
   The War of 1812 / Simon Adams.

(Uncovering the past: analyzing primary sources)
Includes bibliographical references and index.
Issued in print and electronic formats.
ISBN 978-0-7787-4800-7 (hardcover).--
ISBN 978-0-7787-4826-7 (softcover).--
ISBN 978-1-4271-2089-2 (HTML)

   1. United States--History--War of 1812--Juvenile literature.
2. Canada--History--War of 1812--Juvenile literature. 3. United
States--History--War of 1812--Sources--Juvenile literature. 4.
Canada--History--War of 1812--Sources--Juvenile literature. I.
Title.

E354.A33 2018   j973.5'2   C2017-907715-5
                                          C2017-907716-3

Library of Congress Cataloging-in-Publication Data

Names: Adams, Simon, 1955- author.
Title: The War of 1812 / Simon Adams.
Description: New York : Crabtree Publishing, 2018. |
   Series: Uncovering the past: analyzing primary sources |
   Includes bibliographical references and index.
Identifiers: LCCN 2017057928 (print) | LCCN 2017058309 (ebook) |
   ISBN 9781427120892 (Electronic) |
   ISBN 9780778748007 (hardcover : alk. paper) |
   ISBN 9780778748267 (pbk. : alk. paper)
Subjects: LCSH: United States--History--War of 1812--Juvenile
   literature.
Classification: LCC E354 (ebook) | LCC E354 .A25 2018 (print) |
   DDC 973.5/2--dc23
LC record available at https://lccn.loc.gov/2017057928

Crabtree Publishing Company

www.crabtreebooks.com   1-800-387-7650

Printed in the U.S.A./022018/CG20171220

Published in Canada
Crabtree Publishing
616 Welland Ave.
St. Catharines, ON
L2M 5V6

Published in the United States
Crabtree Publishing
PMB 59051
350 Fifth Avenue, 59th Floor
New York, NY 10118

Published in the United Kingdom
Crabtree Publishing
Maritime House
Basin Road North, Hove
BN41 1WR

Published in Australia
Crabtree Publishing
3 Charles Street
Coburg North
VIC, 3058

UNCOVERING THE PAST

THE PAST COMES ALIVE

"We wish and hope for peace but must be prepared for war. We are engaged in an awful and eventful contest."

Major General Isaac Brock, British military leader, 1812

The War of 1812 was a conflict between the United States of America and Great Britain, including its **provinces** in British North America, now part of modern Canada. The United States declared war on Britain to grow its trade, free North America from British influence, and to gain land for U.S. settlers.

The war was fought in Upper Canada (now Ontario) and Lower Canada (now Quebec), on the Great Lakes, the Atlantic Ocean, and in the United States. It lasted more than two and a half years and left several thousand people dead. Battles were fought, lost, and won by soldiers both on land and at sea. Ordinary people were involved, too, protecting their land, supporting their forces, and struggling to survive in the turmoil.

By the end of the war in early 1815, there were no outright winners and little had changed in North America. Those that suffered most were the **Indigenous peoples**, many of whom became allies of the British with the hope of halting American settler expansion into their territory.

How do we know what caused the War of 1812, what happened in the battles and skirmishes, and what is the **legacy** of the war? We can find out these things from the **evidence** created and gathered at the time and from the material produced afterward to document the events. This book looks at the variety and different types of evidence of the war and how it was viewed in the past, and **analyzed** today. Our view of the war today is shaped by historians—people who uncover and interpret the past and help us understand how to avoid such conflicts in the future.

▶ Early on in the war, U.S. sailors on the ship U.S.S. *Constitution* prepare to fire cannon on the British ship H.M.S. *Guerriere*.

DEFINITIONS

A **colony** is a country or territory under the rule or control of another and where settlers live. The original 13 U.S. states on the East Coast of North America were once British colonies. A province is part of one country, sometimes ruled by another country, with its own government.

Britian's territories in Canada, then called British North America, were divided into Upper and Lower Canada and the colonies of Cape Breton Island, Nova Scotia, New Brunswick, Prince Edward Island, and Newfoundland. A **territory** is a part of a country governed by another, distant, part.

ANALYZE THIS

What do you notice about the age and uniforms of the sailors? What makes you think the sailors are prepared for battle? What weapons do they have? How might they use swords in a sea battle?

EVIDENCE OF A WAR

How do you remember events that have happened to you? Do family pictures help you remember a vacation, a birthday party, or the birth of a brother or sister? Did you keep tickets from a sports event or a visit to a theme park to help jog your memory? Perhaps you sent and kept a message to a friend detailing what you did and how you felt at the time. All of these things and many others help you collect your memories of past events and determine the highs—and perhaps some lows—of your childhood. If one day you wanted to write an autobiography—a history of your life—these are the documents you would use.

Major events, such as the War of 1812, shaped the lives of the people involved in the same way. Those people had their own accounts and memories. Some of them may have documented their experiences in diaries, reports, and sketches. Historians look for these materials and use them to build up a picture of the war. Looking back at things that have happened in the past is an important step in understanding the **culture** and beliefs of our ancestors. This understanding can be used to guide and

▼ In a War of 1812 reenactment of the siege of Fort Erie in the summer of 1814, American troops fire on British forces.

influence how we live today so that wars and other human catastrophes can be avoided in the future.

Each historian has a different reason for uncovering and analyzing the story of the War of 1812. One may want to write biographies of the generals, admirals, and soldiers involved. Another may be interested in the fighting strategies and tactics used in the battles. A third historian may want to find out how Indigenous peoples were affected. Yet another may want to write a children's book about how life may have been for boys and girls caught up in the war. Historians try to find and analyze a wide variety of documents about the past as each piece of evidence is a unique view and interpretation about what may, or may not, have happened at the time.

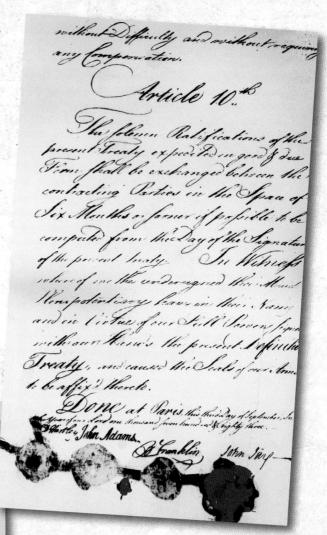

EVIDENCE RECORD CARD

Treaty of Paris, signed by John Adams, Benjamin Franklin, and others

LEVEL Primary source
MATERIAL Handwritten document
LOCATION Paris, France
DATES September 3, 1783
SOURCE Library of Congress/ALAMY

▲ The Treaty of Paris 1783, under which Britain recognized U.S. independence from its rule.

"That these united Colonies are, and of Right ought to be Free and Independent States, that they are Absolved from all Allegiance to the British Crown, and that all political connection between them and the State of Great Britain, is and ought to be totally dissolved; and that as Free and Independent States, they have full Power to levy War, conclude Peace, contract Alliances, establish Commerce, and to do all other Acts and Things which Independent States may of right do."

From the U.S. Declaration of Independence, signed on July 4, 1776

TYPES OF EVIDENCE

"The challenge of history is to recover the past and introduce it to the future."

American historian David Thelen, 1989

In human history, "the past" may be only days, weeks, or months ago, or it can refer to many hundreds or thousands of years back in time. In the case of the War of 1812, which lasted from June 1812 to February 1815, it is more than 200 years ago. Some historians study the ancient past, others recent events.

Each period, age, or era of history has its own mix of sources of evidence available. A source is a place you get information. It could be an archaeological dig site, a person, an **archive**, or a record book. Modern sources of historical information include textbooks, websites, sound recordings, photographs, and documentary films.

For the War of 1812, sources include battle plans, diaries, journals, newspaper articles, paintings, **broadsides**, letters, and flags like those illustrated in this book. At that time, there was no photography, video cameras, audio equipment, telephones, or computers. Battle sites were later cleared of dead bodies, weapons, and other evidence, so little or nothing remains to be seen where the events happened.

Historians of the War of 1812 gather material from as many different sources as they can. They study, read, and analyze the evidence and understand what took place, and why, when, and where it happened. They build up a picture of the politics, **economy**, and ambitions of the United States, Great Britain, and British North America, and the goals of Indigenous peoples. They try to explain to ordinary people the importance of history and how it can provide lessons and guidance for how governments work today.

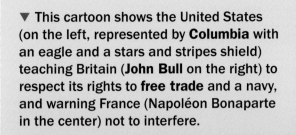

▼ This cartoon shows the United States (on the left, represented by **Columbia** with an eagle and a stars and stripes shield) teaching Britain (**John Bull** on the right) to respect its rights to **free trade** and a navy, and warning France (Napoléon Bonaparte in the center) not to interfere.

PRIMARY EVIDENCE

There are two main sources of historical evidence—primary and secondary. **Primary sources** are firsthand accounts or **artifacts**, or objects, created at the time an event happened. They include reports made by people who witnessed or took part in the event and the remains of incidents of the time such as the ruins of buildings hit by cannon fire. Primary sources from the War of 1812 include **treaties**, or agreements, like the ones shown on page 7 and here. Maps created during battles are another primary source: See page 30 for an example. Many of the quotes and statements used in this book are a third category of primary sources. Primary sources can be things that were written, recorded as images or as auditory, or sound, messages, or objects made at the time, such as weapons.

Written primary sources include:

- Diaries: Books in which people document their personal thoughts
- Journals: Books in which people log details about specific events, activities, or trips

▶ This is the 1803 treaty with France agreeing to the Louisiana Purchase, by which the United States doubled its size.

PERSPECTIVES

The Louisiana Purchase treaty was made between the U.S. and French governments without them asking their **citizens** for their views on the matter. How do you feel when your government acts in a similar way? Is acting in this way part of **democracy**?

(Original)

Treaty
Between the United States of America
and the French Republic

- Transcripts: Written text versions of speeches, meetings, and interviews
- Letters: Documents sent between people
- Telegrams: Messages sent over long distances using wire signals that are decoded and written down
- Lyrics: Words to songs that people sing
- Blogs: Online journals
- Social media: Posts and updates on public websites

The War of 1812 was a conflict between several countries, each with its own government, laws, and language. It is therefore rich in the variety of written primary sources. Today, many of these can be seen in museums, libraries, and government offices.

Visual primary sources include:
- Photographs: Images created on film and printed on paper or stored on disk
- Paintings: Images made on canvas with paint

- Maps: Diagrams of a region or area
- Videos and movies: Moving images recorded by cameras
- Political cartoons: Images drawn by an illustrator to make a point, with or without words
- Physical objects such as coins, weapons, pottery, knives, and flags

Visual items are images or objects made by people directly or with the help of technology. Images of events, places, and people involved in the War of 1812 were captured by artists. Their paintings, sketches, political cartoons, and engravings give us evidence of the past by showing us the traditions, fashions, and reactions to events long ago. Many of these illustrate this book.

▶ Josiah Quincy III—shown here in a cartoon of 1813—was a U.S. politician who opposed the War of 1812. The letters he wrote and speeches he gave at the time are primary sources, but this image is a **secondary source** (see pages 12–13).

"We have lived long, but this is the noblest work of our whole lives. . . From this day the United States take their place among the powers of the first rank."

Robert Livingston, a U.S. signatory of the Louisiana Purchase, 1803

AUDITORY PRIMARY SOURCES

"Auditory" means relating to sound. Recordings of speeches or interviews are auditory sources, as are music and songs. Auditory sources let us hear and share the memories and experiences of people who lived through events in their own voice. Emotions such as fear, sadness, and relief can be heard in how they speak or even cry. Folk songs, ballads, and rap songs all tell stories. The most well-known song telling a story of the War of 1812 is "The Star-Spangled Banner," the national anthem of the United States (see pages 13 and 29).

SECONDARY SOURCES

A good deal of history is secondhand: it is based on sources of evidence made long after the events to which it relates. Secondary sources are often created by looking at, or evaluating, primary sources such as letters, maps, journals, and diaries. Paintings and cartoons that illustrate or visualize a certain moment in history are considered secondary sources.

PERSPECTIVES

How are the individuals represented in this image, created in 1777? What impression do you think the artist was trying to give? What role might the person kneeling play?

◀ Before the War of 1812, Britain and France traded freely for furs with the Indigenous peoples of North America.

"We shall drive the British from our continent—they will no longer have an opportunity of intriguing with our Indian neighbors, and setting on the ruthless savage to tomahawk our women and children. That nation will lose her Canadian trade, and, by having no resting place in this country, her means of annoying us will be diminished."

Congressman Felix Grundy of Tennessee, speaking in the House of Representatives, 1811

Secondary sources can include:

- Newspaper and magazine articles: Writing that focuses on a topic
- Novels: Fictional books with characters and events that often mirror reality to a certain degree
- Textbooks: Books containing facts and figures that are used to teach and learn
- Movies: Re-creations of events using actors and actresses and often reconstructions of buildings and battlesites
- Encyclopedias: Books or websites that give a little information about many subjects. These are often written by teams of historians and experts and are often regarded as "tertiary (third-level) sources"
- Interviews: Discussions with witnesses or with experts who did not participate in the events
- Paintings: Artists' interpretations of events

EVIDENCE RECORD CARD

Cover of sheet music for "The Star-Spangled Banner"

LEVEL Secondary source
MATERIAL Colored engraving on paper
PUBLISHER William Dressler
DATE About 1861
SOURCE Library of Congress

▲ A portrait of Francis Scott Key, who wrote the lyrics of the song.

▶ Cover for sheet music of the U.S. national anthem (see page 29).

DIFFERENCES BETWEEN SOURCES

To determine if a source is primary or secondary, ask yourself these questions:

- Did the author or creator get their information from someone else's work instead of personal experience?
- Is the creator interpreting events or drawing conclusions instead of giving facts?
- Is the date of the work long after the event?

If the answer to any of these is "yes," the source is almost certainly secondary.

With some sources, the dividing line is not always obvious. A war artist's illustration of a battle scene made during the conflict is a primary source, but one he or she created later using sketches and photographs from the time is a secondary source. An interview 10 years after the battle with a soldier who fought in it is a primary source as it is a firsthand account.

Primary sources are generally considered to be more **accurate** and representative of what took place. That is because they are firsthand, or made by people involved in the event. Most of them are not based on memories. Those that are can be misleading. For example, it is well documented that people who witness a crime often fail to identify the

PERSPECTIVES

What source material might the illustrator have used to create this battle scene for a U.S. children's history book of 1922?

THE YOUTH'S COMPANION HISTORIC MILESTONES

 THE BATTLE OF NEW ORLEANS NOT ONLY RAISED ANDREW JACKSON · THEN A LITTLE KNOWN SOUTHERNER · TO THE HIGHEST RANK OF MILITARY AND POLITICAL IMPORTANCE · BUT ENDED FOREVER THE DANGER THAT A FOREIGN POWER MIGHT DOMINATE THE MISSISSIPPI VALLEY

"Don't deceive yourselves; do not believe that all the nations of Indians united are able to resist the force of the Seventeen Fires [the then 17 states of the United States]. I know your warriors are brave, but ours are not less so; but what can a few brave warriors do, against the innumerable warriors of the Seventeen Fires?"

William Henry Harrison, 1803

▲ U.S. Army Major General Andrew Jackson's forces fought the British at the Battle of New Orleans in 1815, the last major battle of the War of 1812.

offender in a police line-up. In the action and chaos of the event, the witness probably was not focusing on such an important detail.

People who create or find primary and secondary sources do so for particular reasons. It may be to accurately record what happened so that others later can share their experiences or honor brave actions, or to ensure such events never happen again. Each witness, reporter, recorder, or analyzer of the event will have his or her own interpretation of the facts. This is known as **bias**. Views on the War of 1812 differed for American, British, and British North American soldiers and for the Indigenous peoples, as discussed in the next chapter.

▲ A portrait of William Henry Harrison, who became the ninth U.S. president in 1841.

▼ This scene from the Battle of Tippecanoe on November 7, 1811, was created in about 1889. It shows Shawnee warriors led by Tenskwatawa—the brother of Tecumseh, the Shawnee Chief—fighting U.S. forces led by William Henry Harrison. The Shawnee were defeated but took revenge when they sided with the British during the War of 1812 (see page 36).

INTERPRETATION

"Who does not know that the first law of historical writing is the truth."

Cicero, Roman politician and lawyer, in about 63 B.C.

Each of the participants in the War of 1812—the United States, Great Britain, British North America, and the Indigenous peoples of North America—had strong and differing views on their rights to land, trade, and liberty. Their views shaped how they reported on the build up to the war, the battles, and their outcomes. Historians regard many of these reports as biased. A biased source tries to change someone's viewpoint, opinion, or **perspective** on a topic.

Bias is when one side of a story is tilted in favor of another or when supporting facts and figures are used in an imbalanced way. If a source is biased, the creator has expressed an opinion for or against a certain person, group, or thing. People who create primary and secondary sources may show bias by including some of their personal feelings or beliefs in the source. If a source is **credible**, it will be fact-based and impartial. There are things historians look for that indicate a source is biased:

- Omitted facts
- Positive or negative word choices
- Additional, unnecessary details
- Extreme language
- Emotional connections
- Political views of the creator

Recognizing and dealing with this bias is part of the story of the War of 1812 and our understanding of how it shaped North America.

▼ This cartoon of 1813 makes fun of U.S. soldiers marching toward Canada to attack British forces there. It was thought—wrongly—that the conflict would be so easy that the soldiers could take their wives, children, pets, and household goods with them.

ANALYZE THIS

Among those defending the British colonies in Canada were untrained **militia** and Indigenous **allies**. How do you think these people felt having to fight trained U.S. soldiers? Why do you think they were often victorious in battles with U.S. forces?

SOLDIERS on a march to BUFFALO.

THE IMPORTANCE OF CONTEXT

Historians must take special care when analyzing **source materials**. They consider the following factors when deciding if a document, image, or artifact offers accurate information about a particular time in history:

- What type of evidence is it—image, transcript—and what does it tell you?
- Who created it—what do you know about this person's credibility?
- When was it created—how long after the event?
- What was happening in the world at the time when it was created?

- What point of view does it represent—the author's, the victim's, simple facts?
- How does the point of view shape the source?

It is generally believed that the best sources of historical information are those created closest in time and place to an event or situation. Also, sources that contradict commonly accepted facts or information may be less credible. Historians must consider **context**, too—the circumstances or setting in which a source was created. Context influences people's outlook or perspective. For example, during and after the **American Revolutionary War** of 1775 to 1783, many Americans moved north to settle

▼ This 1859 painting of the Battle of Lundy's Lane of July 25, 1814, shows the U.S. Army fighting British troops to a standstill with 850 men killed or wounded on each side.

in British North America (now Canada). These people were called Loyalists or the King's Loyal Americans, because they stayed loyal to Great Britain and its king, George III. They did not believe that the United States would treat them well. One Loyalist, Reverend Mather Byles, said, "Which is better—to be ruled by one **tyrant** three thousand miles away [Britain] or by three thousand tyrants one mile away [the revolutionary colonists]?"

Historians of the war might compare the loyalists' perspective with those of Indigenous peoples. A Shawnee tribe member might have a similar perspective to the loyalists, because the Shawnee were also allied with Britain and they fought against the U.S. settlement of their lands. On the other hand, the perspective of an American soldier is likely to show support for U.S. settlement and a negative view of Britain.

Stop, Stop Stop Brother Jonathan. or I shall fall with the loss of blood— I thought to have been too heavy for you— But I must acknowledge your superior skill. Two blows to my one!— And so well directed too! Mercy, mercy on me, how does this happen!!!

Ha—ah Johnny! you thought yourself a Boxer did you!—I'll let you know we are an Enterprizeing Nation, and ready to meet you with equal force any day.

W. Charles del et Sculp

A BOXING MATCH, or Another Bloody Nose f

▲ A cartoon about a naval battle in the war, with Britain's King George III—with a bloody nose— sparring with U.S. President James Madison.

"Facts are stubborn things; and whatever may be our wishes ... they cannot alter the state of facts and evidence."

John Adams, 1770

ANALYZE THIS

How accurate a view of history is this cartoon? Do you think it reflects what really happened during the War of 1812, or was the artist just trying to be humorous?

THE WAR OF 1812

"It has become manifest to every attentive observer, that the early and continued aggressions of Great Britain on our persons, our property, and our rights, imperiously demand a firm stand . . ."

U.S. Secretary of State James Madison
in a public letter, dated January 5, 1804

After the Revolutionary War, in 1783 the 13 united colonies that had declared their independence signed the Treaty of Paris. But relations between the United States and Great Britain remained tense. The U.S. border with British-controlled Canada stayed in dispute—it was not finally settled until 1846—while the British still occupied their military forts in Michigan, New York, and Ohio. The British used these forts as trading posts with the Wyandot, Delaware, Shawnee, Chippewa, and other Indigenous peoples. The British traded guns, blankets, tools, and alcohol for the fur pelts of beaver, mink, and racoon hunted and trapped by the Indigenous peoples. They sold the pelts in Europe.

In addition to this trade, the British and Indigenous peoples remained allies for other reasons. American settlement was expanding, and Great Britain wanted to maintain control over British North America. At the same time, Indigenous peoples wanted to protect their land from American settlers. As it was also in Great Britain's interest to stop American settler expansion, they supported the Indigenous peoples' aims by giving them guns. When Americans tried to settle the **Northwest Territory**, they often fought against Indigenous peoples who protected their land using British weapons. The Americans felt it was time for Great Britain to fully honor U.S. independence and stay out of its internal affairs.

▼ In this scene during 1786, American colonists are rising up against their British rulers. The villagers are seen raising a liberty pole to claim their freedom, although some people appear to disagree with this action. In the background, several men are removing a sign bearing the likeness of George III, the British king.

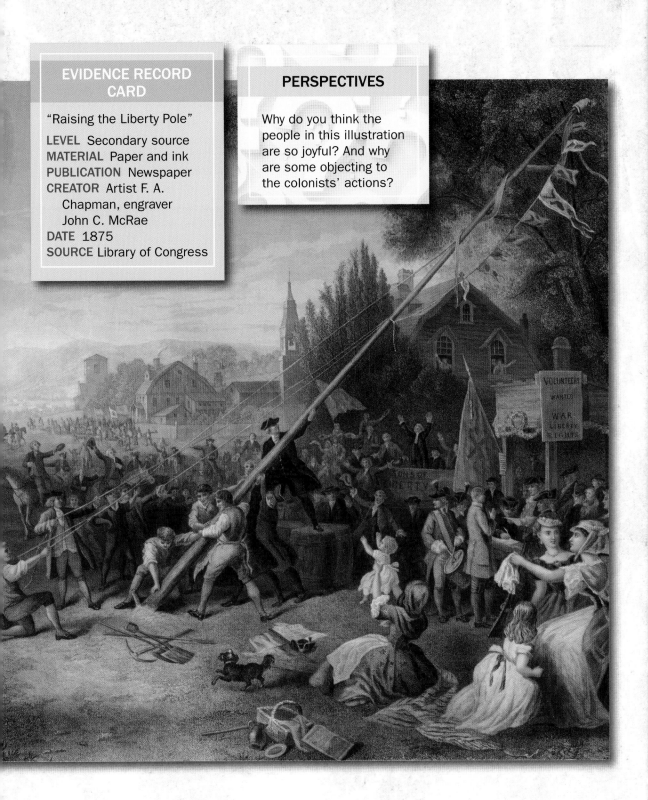

PERSPECTIVES

Why do you think the people in this illustration are so joyful? And why are some objecting to the colonists' actions?

THE FRENCH WARS

In 1789, the French **Revolution** began. The French people rose in revolt against their government, overthrew their king Louis XVI, whom they executed in 1793, and declared a **republic**. France then declared war on its neighbors, including Britain. The two nations would now be at war almost continuously until 1815.

At first, Britain's war with France was good news for the United States. It remained **neutral** in the war and did not favor either side. Its merchants profitably shipped goods to both sides. This good fortune did not last. Both Britain and France cut off the other's trade by **blockading** each other's ports. U.S. **exports** collapsed. In 1807, the U.S. **Congress** responded by passing the Embargo Act, which prevented the United States from trading with all other countries. The idea behind this act was to starve France and Britain of U.S. goods and money. This would then make them stop interfering with U.S. trade.

Britain also began to **impress**, or legally force, sailors to join its navy. The British Royal Navy was superior to that of France, but it needed 114,000 seamen to service its ships, and casualties in battle were high. A seaman's pay was low and the conditions dangerous, so many sailors deserted their ships and worked in the navies of other countries, including that

▼ During the **Napoleonic Wars**, U.S. sailors were taken from their ships by British sailors and forced against their wishes to fight for the British Royal Navy.

of the United States. The British responded by stopping U.S. ships at sea to reclaim their former sailors. Some of these sailors were now U.S. citizens. It is estimated that about 5,000 legitimate U.S. citizens were impressed from their ships between 1793 and 1812.

Matters came to a head in 1807. The U.S. navy **frigate** *Chesapeake*, sailing off the coast of Norfolk, Virginia, included many former British sailors in its crew. On June 22 the British frigate H.M.S. *Leopard* approached the *Chesapeake*. Its commander requested to board the U.S. ship and search for British deserters. Captain James Barron of the *Chesapeake* refused, at which point H.M.S. *Leopard* opened fire, killing three men and wounding 16. British sailors then boarded the *Chesapeake* and removed four men, three of whom were deserters but U.S. citizens. In 1811, Britain apologized to the United States for the attack, but many Americans were outraged by the incident and by impressment. Some members of Congress called for war.

ANALYZE THIS

Do you think the British Royal Navy was right to impress U.S. sailors to fight in its ranks? Why or why not? Was this policy necessary because Britain was at war with France, or was it **piracy**?

▶ This newspaper article printed in Boston, Massachusetts, on March 25, 1808, protested **against the British attack on the U.S. navy frigate** *Chesapeake* **the previous year. The newspaper accused the British of piracy.**

British Barbarity and Piracy !!

THE LEAD UP TO WAR

Unfortunately, the Embargo Act hurt the U.S. economy. Farmers could not sell their crops, and ship owners and sailors lost their jobs. In 1809, Congress replaced the act with the Non-Intercourse Act. This allowed the United States to trade with all nations except France and Britain. If either nation stopped seizing U.S. ships and sailors, the United States would resume trade with it. In 1810, France promised to respect U.S. shipping, but the British government refused.

In 1809, James Madison became U.S. president. He hoped to stop British interference with U.S. shipping in a peaceful way. However, many members of Congress called for war. These congressmen were nicknamed the "War Hawks." They wanted a war to stop British interference with U.S. trade and shipping; to stop the British from supplying Indigenous peoples with guns used to defend their

PERSPECTIVES

This document from the U.S. **Senate** records shows the various **amendments** made to the original declaration of war proposal. Why do you think these changes were made? Do you think they strengthened the original proposal?

▶ A draft bill declaring war on Britain was debated in the U.S. Senate on June 17, 1812. War was officially declared the next day.

land against U.S. settlers, and to remind Britain and the world that the United States had won its freedom in 1776 and must defend that freedom.

The War Hawks felt that victory would be easy. While Britain had many ships, it did not have enough soldiers to protect its lands in Canada. The United States could then occupy that country and use it as a bargaining chip to end Britain's interference in shipping.

Gradually the War Hawks gained support. On June 1, 1812, President Madison gave in. He asked Congress to declare war on Britain. The British government acted to calm the situation. It did not want to fight another war while the war with France was still raging. It could not spare either the soldiers or the ships to fight the United States. On June 16, 1812, just two days before Congress was to vote on war, the British foreign secretary Lord Castlereagh proposed to cancel the order that prevented trade with the United States. The change of heart was too late, for the news took five weeks to cross the Atlantic Ocean. By then, the two countries were at war.

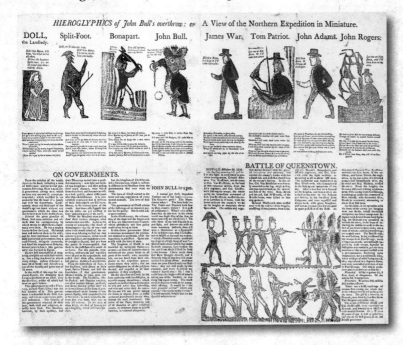

◄ This U.S. broadside was probably printed in New York State. It reported on the U.S. defeat of the British at Queenston Heights in Ontario, Canada, on October 13, 1812, one of the first major battles of the war.

"...Have they not in congress, in our own State Legislature, and in all other public bodies openly avowed their attachment to the government of Great Britain, and their cruel, unjust, and unnatural opposition to our own? ... AMERICANS, Rouse from your slumbers! A desperate attempt is making on your liberties. Let another year pass, without counteracting the horid evils which impend over you, and the voice of warning may be too late..."

The Voice of Warning! issued by War Hawks in New York in 1810

THE WAR IN THE GREAT LAKES

The initial U.S. war plan was to invade Upper and Lower Canada. U.S. troops led by General William Hull soon crossed the Detroit River, but on hearing that Fort Mackinac in northern Michigan had already fallen to the British, they retreated back across the river to Detroit. There they met a British army led by Major General Sir Isaac Brock with support from the Shawnee, led by Tecumseh, and other Indigenous peoples. Tecumseh had united different Indigenous peoples to create a **confederacy**. He believed that the best way to protect Indigenous land from American settlement was to join together and support the British in the war. Believing himself to be heavily outnumbered, Hull surrendered on August 16, 1812, opening up the Northwest Territory to the British.

The first significant battle of the War of 1812 took place on October 13, 1812, when a large U.S. force crossed the Niagara River, overwhelming the British and killing their commander, Major General Brock, at Queenston Heights. However, the arrival of British reinforcements, as well as about 100 **Six Nations**

ANALYZE THIS

Almost 5,000 troops fought the Battle of Queenston Heights, of which 121 were killed and a further 255 were wounded. Do you think this colorful painting gives a good idea of the ferocity of this battle?

EVIDENCE RECORD CARD

Battle of Queenston Heights

LEVEL Secondary source
MATERIAL Oil on canvas
LOCATION Queenston Heights above the Niagara River, Upper Canada
DATE 1814
SOURCE Alamy

▼ The Battle of Queenston Heights, fought on October 13, 1812, was an important victory for the British.

fighters led by Mohawk chief John Norton, turned the tide of the battle, leading to a hard-fought British victory.

To the west, a U.S. **fleet** on Lake Erie defeated the British on September 10, 1813, depriving them of a vital supply line to both their own troops and to their Indigenous allies. Weeks later, U.S. troops reoccupied Detroit. On October 5, 1813, they engaged the British and their Indigenous allies on the Thames River in Upper Canada. The British were easily defeated, and Tecumseh was killed (see pages 36–37). Without his leadership, Tecumseh's confederacy fell apart. Other Indigenous allies fought on. The June 24, 1813 Battle of Beaverdams was fought exclusively by Kahnawake (Mohawks) against Americans.

The war in the Great Lakes region then swung back and forth. On July 25, 1814, a U.S. attack on Niagara was stopped at at the Battle of Lundy's Lane, one of the bloodiest battles of the war. Weeks later, on September 11, a British fleet was defeated on Lake Champlain, preventing British troops from advancing on New York. Neither side was winning the war.

▶ Victory at the Battle of Lake Champlain on September 11, 1814, was a major triumph for the U.S. Navy and prevented the British from attacking New York. This engraving of the fighting was created a few years after the battle.

"We should have to fight hereafter, not for 'free trade and sailors' rights,' not for the conquest of the Canadas, but for our national existence."

U.S. Captain Joseph Hopper Nicholson, May 20, 1814

THE ATLANTIC BLOCKADE

At the start of the war, the British believed that the U.S. Navy was no match for the Royal Navy. The United States had fewer ships, although these were more powerful than most British ships. However, the U.S. sailors were all volunteers, with better pay and conditions than their impressed British counterparts, and were eager to defend their country. In order to increase their fleets, both sides engaged in **privateering**, or outfitting private merchant ships to attack and capture enemy ships. Successful privateers often captured more than 50 enemy ships in the war.

British naval confidence was soon struck by the loss of three major warships in battles with U.S. ships. In response, the Royal Navy began to blockade East Coast ports, preventing U.S. trade with Europe and hindering

PERSPECTIVES

What would it be like to come under enemy fire in a ship? Would you feel safe in a wooden-hulled ship, or afraid? How would you feel if you were on board one of the smaller boats?

▶ The U.S. privateer *General Armstrong* opens fire on British boats sent from H.M.S. *Carnation* to capture her during the Battle of Fayal in the Portuguese Azores in the mid-Atlantic on September 26–27, 1814.

"In the United States, every possible encouragement should be given to privateering in time of war with a commercial nations."

Former U.S. President Thomas Jefferson, 1812

◀ President James Madison and, probably, Secretary of War John Armstrong flee the burning buildings of Washington, D.C., in August 1814, carrying bundles of state papers.

efforts to resupply its forces by sea. The blockade was hugely successful, reducing the value of U.S. exports from $130 million in 1807 to about $7 million in 1814 and forcing merchants to ship their goods by lengthier and more costly land routes. About 4,000 **enslaved peoples** took this opportunity to flee and join the British blockading ships or journey north to Canada. Many were encouraged by the British decision to offer them their freedom if they changed sides. Some formerly enslaved peoples joined the new Corps of Colonial Marines and fought successfully in the war.

In retaliation for U.S. attacks on Canadian towns, including York (now Toronto), British forces under Major General Robert Ross attacked Washington, D.C., the U.S. capital. Troops entered the city with little opposition on August 24, 1814, burning the White House and other government buildings. They then moved on to attack Baltimore. British ships bombarded Fort McHenry on September 13, 1814, but Ross was killed in the action, which was called off after failing to cripple the fort.

◀ After the bombardment of Fort McHenry ended on September 14, 1814, local lawyer Francis Scott Key wrote a poem called "The Star-Spangled Banner." Set to music, the poem became the U.S. national anthem.

THE WAR IN THE SOUTH

Following a major victory over the French in Europe in 1814, the British could now devote many more ships and troops to their fight against the United States. They now planned a major assault against the southern United States, securing the mouth of the Mississippi River and thus severing a major U.S. trade route. The United States anticipated the assault and sent Andrew Jackson to prepare the defenses of New Orleans.

In December 1814, a British fleet under Vice-Admiral Sir Alexander Cochrane arrived off New Orleans. It then wasted three days rounding up seven U.S. ships before landing troops. Jackson used this time to

PERSPECTIVES

The battles of New Orleans and Fort Bowyer were fought in the south of the United States in early 1815. How important were these battles, considering that the War of 1812 was already over?

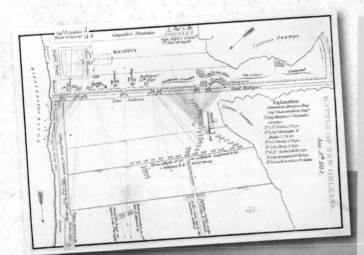

◄ This primary-source map shows the positions of the two armies during the Battle of New Orleans on January 8, 1815.

▼ During the Battle of New Orleans, British troops under General Edward Pakenham lined up against U.S. troops led by Major-General Andrew Jackson. The Mississippi River is in the foreground. This illustration was created at the time by a French engraver.

build up his defenses. Jackson took up position alongside the Rodriguez Canal and built a **rampart** of logs, mud, and cotton bales behind which he set up his artillery. The first British assault on December 28 under General Edward Pakenham was called off when his supplies ran low, but the two sides finally engaged each other on January 8, 1815. The British intended to advance in the early morning fog, but their passage was slow and the fog had lifted by the time they emerged on the battlefield, making them easy targets for U.S. riflemen. General Pakenham and his deputy were both killed, and the British soldiers were mown down in front of Jackson's ramparts. Eventually, the British retreated to their ships.

Undeterred, the British then set off to capture Fort Bowyer in Mobile Bay. This they achieved on February 11, 1815. Two days after its fall, H.M.S. *Brazen* arrived with word that the war had been over since December 24, 1814.

▼ In a print of 1892, Major General Andrew Jackson, shown here on a white horse, used the days before the battle to build up defenses and gather together enough troops in New Orleans. This was crucial in winning the battle.

"At the close of Major Villere's narrative the General drew up his figure, bowed with disease and weakness, to its full height, and with an eye of fire and an emphatic blow upon the table with his clenched fist, exclaimed: 'By the Eternal, they shall not sleep on our soil!'"

Stanley Clisby Arthur, *The Story of the Battle of New Orleans*, 1915

THE END OF THE WAR

By the middle of 1814, both sides in the War of 1812 realized that neither side was winning. Therefore they set up talks with each other, starting in July 1814 in the city of Ghent, then part of the Austrian Netherlands and now in Belgium. Both negotiating teams were given unrealistic instructions from their governments. The U.S. delegation was told to demand both Upper and Lower Canada from the British. The British delegation, expecting large numbers of troops to arrive in Canada from Europe shortly, was told to keep that part of northern Maine that interfered with the trade route from New Brunswick into Quebec and Lower Canada. The British also wanted to establish a territory for their Indigenous allies west of the Mississippi River.

Negotiations dragged on for several months until pressures on both sides forced their diplomats to work harder for a settlement. The British were worried that war could restart in Europe, as indeed it did before Napoléon was finally defeated at the Battle of Waterloo in June 1815. In the meantime, the U.S. economy was collapsing thanks to the British naval blockade. The U.S. delegates were also worried about talk of the New England states leaving the Union to form their own confederacy.

◀ **British and U.S. diplomats shake hands in Ghent on December 24, 1814, having signed a peace treaty to end the War of 1812.**

ANALYZE THIS

How do you think the two sets of diplomats viewed each other at Ghent? What group is missing from this picture?

"I think you have no right, from the state of war, to demand any concession of territory from America. . . You have not been able to carry it into the enemy's territory, notwithstanding your military success, and now undoubted military superiority, and have not even cleared your own territory on the point of attack. You cannot on any principle of equality in negotiation claim a cession of territory except in exchange for other advantages which you have in your power. . ."

The Duke of Wellington, Great Britain, 1814

By mid-November 1814, both sides were eager to put the war behind them. They agreed that the U.S.–Canada border should be restored to what it was before the war began. The final details took more time to work out, but the peace treaty was finally agreed on December 24, 1814. The official end to the war came on February 16, 1815, when the U.S. Senate formally **ratified** the treaty.

Fighting continued in the United States for several weeks following ratification, as word of the treaty took time to get out from Ghent and cross the Atlantic by ship to reach the various armies on the ground.

▼ **Signatures and wax seals on the Treaty of Ghent indicated agreement from both sides to end the war.**

A WAR OF DIVISION

"For Canadians, the War of 1812 was about American invasions. For Americans, it was about standing up to Britain. For the British, it was an annoying sideshow to the Napoleonic Wars. For Indigenous people, it was a desperate struggle for freedom and independence as they fought to defend their homelands."

Canadian historian D. Peter MacLeod, 2012

The War of 1812 was often referred to as "the war both sides won." Both the United States and British North America—now Canada—had claimed it as a victory. The British and their allies had successfully repelled several invasions of their territory. The Americans had reasserted sovereignty, or control over their territory. It was considered a "second War of Independence," for they had once again fought the British and not given up any land.

Support for the War of 1812 was not always straightforward at the time. In Lower Canada, the rural French population was concerned that crops would not be harvested if men were forced to spend time away in militias. Politicians questioned whether they would defend against American invasions. But French civil laws, customs, religion, and language were protected in Lower Canada, and people did not feel they would be if taken over by the United States.

On the U.S. side, many of its citizens wanted peace, notably the farmers who could not sell their crops and merchants who could not trade their goods. But War Hawks argued to declare war on Great Britain and to invade Canada. They thought Canada would be easy pickings.

Indigenous peoples had hopes of maintaining control over their own land and forming alliances of equals with the United States and Great Britain.

▼ In this 19th-century painting, the crew of the victorious U.S. frigate U.S.S. *Constitution* fire on the badly damaged British ship H.M.S. *Guerriere*, disabling the ship.

▶ This broadside, printed in Boston in 1812, celebrates the victory of the *Constitution* over H.M.S. *Guerriere* on August 19, 1812.

CONSTITUTION AND GUERRIERE.

BRITANNIA's gallant streamers
Float proudly o'er the tide;
And fairly wave Columbia's stripes,
In battle side by side,
And ne'er did bolder foemen meet,
Where ocean's surges pour,
O'er the tide, now they ride,
While the bell'wing thunders roar,
While the cannon's fire is flashing fast,
And the bell'wing thunders roar.

When Yankee meets the Briton,
Whose blood congenial flows,
By heaven created to be friends,
By fortune render'd foes;
Hard then must be the battle fray,
Ere well the fight is o'er.
Now they ride, side by side,
While the bell'wing thunders roar,
While the cannon's fire is flashing fast,
And the bell'wing thunders roar.

Still, still, for noble England,
Bold DACRES' streamers fly;
And for Columbia, gallant HULL's,
As proudly and as high,
Now loudly rings the battle din,
More thick the volumes pour;
Still they ride, side by side,
While the bell'wing thunders roar,
While the cannon's fire is flashing fast,
And the bell'wing thunders roar.

Why lulls Britannia's thunder,
That wak'd the watery war?
Why stays the gallant Guerriere,
Whose streamer wav'd so fair?
That streamer drink' th' ocean wave!
That warrior's fight 's o'er!
Still they ride, side by side,
While Columbia's thunders roar,
While her cannon's fire is flashing fast,
And her Yankee thunders roar.

Hark! 'tis the Briton's lee gun!
Ne'er bolder warrior kneel'd!
And ne'er to gallant mariners
Did braver seamen yield.
Proud be the sires whose hardy boys,
Then fell, to fight no more;
With the brave, mid the wave,
When the cannon's thunders roar,
Their spirits then shall trim the blast,
And swell the thunder's roar.

Vain were the cheers of Britons,
Their hearts did vainly swell,
Where virtue, skill and bravery,
With gallant Morris fell.
That heart so well in battle tri'd,
Along the Moorish shore,
Again, o'er the main,
When Columbia's thunders roar,
Shall prove its Yankee spirit true,
When Columbia's thunders roar.

Hence be our floating bulwarks,
Those oaks our mountains yield;
'Tis mighty Heaven's plain decree—
Then take the wat'ry field!
To ocean's farthest barrier then
Your whit'ning sail shall pour;
Safe they'll ride, o'er the tide,
While Columbia's thunders roar,
While her cannon's fire is flashing fast,
And her Yankee thunders roar.

PERSPECTIVES

Although naval victories, such as the one illustrated on this page, undoubtedly cheered the United States, the truth was that Britain ruled the waves, enforcing a painful economic blockade of their country. How do you think U.S. citizens felt about this war?

WHO LOST OUT?

For the Indigenous nations of North America, the War of 1812 ended their dream of securing land they could share and preserving their traditional way of life.

Before the war, Indigenous peoples fought white settlers encroaching, or intruding, on their land. Two Shawnee leaders, Tecumseh and his brother, Tenskwatawa (also known as the Prophet), encouraged the Shawnee and other nations, including the Creek, Kickapoo, Menominee, and Osage, to form a confederacy to protect their lands. Tecumseh believed that land was meant to be shared by all people. He was against any one nation selling land meant for all.

In 1808, Tecumseh and Tenskwatawa set up a village named Prophetstown in Indiana. On November 7, 1811, Governor Harrison sent 1,100 troops to attack the village. After Tenskwatawa's men ran out of ammunition, the U.S. troops burned the village to the ground in what is now called the Battle of Tippecanoe.

Fighting between the United States and the Indigenous peoples continued during the war. The Creek Nation of the southeastern United States was divided over whether to live peaceably near the white

▲ On June 21, 1813, Laura Secord overheard U.S. soldiers planning a surprise attack on the British outpost of Beaver Dams in Upper Canada. Her husband had been injured in the war, so the next morning she walked 20 miles (32 km) to warn the British. Two days later, Indigenous allies ambushed the U.S. soldiers and prevented their attack. Secord has become a Canadian heroine, as shown on this postage stamp.

The Peace Memorial on South Bass Island, Ohio, marks a U.S. victory in the Battle of Lake Erie, 1813, and celebrates the lasting peace between Great Britain, Canada, and the United States that followed the War of 1812.

settlers or join Tecumseh's confederacy against U.S. **expansionism**. The White Sticks, led by the older Creek chiefs, favored friendship with the settlers, while the younger Red Sticks fought back. On August 30, 1813, the Red Sticks attacked Fort Mins, killing about 250 U.S. soldiers. In response, on March 27, 1814, Colonel Andrew Jackson led a force of 2,700 West Tennessee militia and **regular infantry**, supported by about 600 Choctaw, Cherokee, and White Sticks fighters, and attacked the Red Stick camp at Horseshoe Bend in Alabama. Jackson's victory was decisive, with most of the

Red Sticks killed. In August 1814, Jackson forced the Creeks to sign the Treaty of Fort Jackson, handing a huge area of land to the U.S. government.

The Treaty of Ghent that ended the war made no reference to the Indigenous peoples. Great Britain abandoned its pledge to establish a territory for them west of the Mississippi River. Their dream of an independent state had died. With no British troops to support them, the Indigenous peoples were now powerless to prevent the westward expansion of the United States across their lands.

▶ It is believed Tecumseh was killed by a pistol shot from Colonel R. M. Johnson on October 5, 1813, during the Battle of the Thames.

"Here is a chance presented to us; yes, such as will never occur again, for us Indians of North America to form ourselves into one great combination, and cast our lot with the British in this war; and should they conquer and again get the mastery of the whole of North America, our rights, at least to a portion of the land of our fathers, would be respected by the King."

Shawnee leader Tecumseh, 1812

HISTORY REPEATED

"The physical treaty, like all things, will eventually fade...But that doesn't mean the commitments that were entered into are completed or are undone."

Kevin Gover (Pawnee), director of the National Museum of the American Indian, January 18, 2015

One clear outcome of the War of 1812 was that the United States and Britain never again went to war with each other or invaded each other's territory. The Treaty of Ghent officially ended a war where neither the United States nor Britain achieved their pre-war aims. No physical territory was handed over and there was no clear winner. By contrast, the groups that lost the most were the Indigenous allies of the British.

In the 1814 treaty negotiations at Ghent, Britain had hoped to secure land in what is modern day Ohio, Indiana, and Michigan for their Indigenous allies. Britain had wanted a **buffer territory** between U.S. land and British territory in Canada. This was rejected by American negotiators as it would prevent westward expansion of the United States—the exact aim that Britain's Indigenous allies had fought against. An article, or section, in the treaty was intended to restore Indigenous lands and rights that existed before 1812. But there was no agreement on what this meant, so it was never put in place. No Indigenous people were present at the treaty negotiations. Tecumseh had thought his alliance with the British was an alliance of equals. The British abandoned him at the Battle of the Thames, and his beliefs and his Confederacy died with him. The British had won many important battles with the support of Indigenous allies, but after the war, they lost interest in supporting their allies' goals. They were no longer needed as military partners.

▼ A monument honoring Tecumseh installed near where he died on the 200th anniversary of the War of 1812. In the U.S. Tecumseh was highly regarded and remembered in poems and art as a defeated foe. In Canada, Tecumseh's ally, British general Sir Isaac Brock had more recognition. Many monuments honor him, and a university in Ontario is named after him.

ALLIES TO WARDS

With no borders or recognized Indigenous territory to stop westward expansion, the decades after the War of 1812 brought more and more settlers into the interior of the United States and Canada. They settled on Indigenous peoples' land. Sometimes, the land was taken by force, and sometimes through treaties. Treaties are accords where Indigenous peoples exchanged some of their interests in the land for payments or promises of continuing care from the government or state.

Treaties were not new—Indigenous peoples had used them among themselves to establish peaceful trading relationships. Much like Tecumseh's view that his military alliance was a relationship of equals, the Indigenous peoples also viewed treaties as solemn pacts between nations where both sides had rights and responsibilities. In treaty negotiations, they believed they were allowing settlers the right to use some of the land, but were not giving up ownership, especially as lands were held in common, or by all Indigenous peoples. By contrast, the state in the United States, and the Crown in Canada, often viewed treaties as a way to end Indigenous ownership of lands and clear the way for settlement. Increased settlement was also intended to assimilate Indigenous peoples. Assimilation was a way of eliminating Indigenous culture by encouraging them to become more like settlers in religion, language, and way of life. In 1830, the United States government passed the Indian Removal Act. This allowed thousands of Indigenous peoples to be forcibly removed from their lands so that the land could be taken by settlers.

▲ Treaties helped make the U.S. and Canada. Treaty medals were sometimes presented to chiefs or leaders who signed treaties. This one shows a representative of the British Crown shaking hands as equals with an Indigenous leader.

"The only way to stop this evil is for all the red men to unite in claiming an equal right in the land. That is how it was at first, and should be still, for the land never was divided, but was for the use of everyone...Sell a country! Why not sell the air, the clouds, and the Great Sea, as well as the earth? Did not the Great Spirit make them all for the use of his children?"

Tecumseh's speech to Governor William Henry Harrison at Vincennes, August 11, 1810.

MORE BROKEN PROMISES

By 1837, roughly 46,000 Indigenous peoples in the U.S. had moved westward—most through force. In one well-known forced removal, known as the Trail of Tears of 1838 to 1839, an estimated 16,000 Indigenous people were marched west. Thousands died on the journey. In areas where treaties were signed, rights were almost immediately ignored or broken to make way for more settlers. In 1871 the U.S. Congress stopped recognizing individual tribes as nations for treaty making.

In Canada, the government signed treaty after treaty to secure Canadian ownership of the land and pave the way for more settlers. In both Canada and the United States, treaties set aside **reservation** lands for Indigenous peoples to live on. These were often remotely located or with poor soil or water, making life there difficult. Indigenous peoples didn't just quietly accept their poor treatment. Just as they resisted encroachment on their territory in 1812, they continue to press governments to adhere to treaties and treat them as equal partners.

◀ Indigenous protestors at a rally. They formed a group called Idle No More to press for more recognition of Indigenous equality and treaty rights.

TIMELINE

1783 Treaty of Paris ends the American Revolutionary War, creating the United States

November 7, 1811 Battle of Tippecanoe

June 18, 1812 United States declares war against Great Britain

July 17, 1812 The British capture Fort Mackinac

August 16, 1812 Surrender of Fort Detroit

October 13, 1812 Battle of Queenston Heights; Major General Isaac Brock is killed

October 25, 1812 U.S.S. *United States* captures H.M.S. *Macedonian*

January 23, 1813 River Raisin Massacre

May 25, 1813 Battle of Fort George begins

June 6, 1813 Battle of Stoney Creek

August 30, 1813 Fort Mims Massacre

September 26, 1813 Harrison retakes Detroit

October 26, 1813 Battle of the Chateauguay

1783

1811

1812

1813

1814

1803 U.S. President Thomas Jefferson's Louisiana Purchase from France means the United States doubles in size

July 12, 1812 U.S. General William Hull invades Canada at Sandwich

August 15, 1812 Fort Dearborn Massacre

August 19, 1812 U.S.S. *Constitution* captures H.M.S. *Guerriere*

October 18, 1812 U.S.S. *Wasp* captures H.M.S. *Frolic*

December 29, 1812 U.S.S. *Constitution* sinks H.M.S. *Java*

April 27, 1813 Battle of York

June 1, 1813 H.M.S. *Shannon* captures U.S.S. *Chesapeake*

June 24, 1813 Battle of Beaver Dams

September 10, 1813 Battle of Lake Erie

October 5, 1813 Battle of the Thames; Tecumseh is killed

November 11, 1813 Battle of Crysler's Farm

December 18, 1813 Recapture of Fort Niagara

March 27, 1814 Battle of Horseshoe Bend

August 4, 1814 Siege of Fort Erie begins

August 24, 1814 Burning of Washington, D.C.

September 13–14, 1814 Bombardment of Fort McHenry

December 15, 1814 Hartford Convention begins

January 8, 1815 Battle of New Orleans

February 16, 1815 Ratified treaties exchanged: War is officially over

1814

July 25, 1814 Battle of Lundy's Lane

August 4, 1814 Battle of Mackinac Island

September 11, 1814 Battle of Lake Champlain (also known as the Battle of Plattsburgh)

September 26–27, 1814 Battle of Fayal

December 24, 1814 Treaty of Ghent is signed

February 11, 1815 British capture Fort Bowyer

1815

The War of 1812—Major territories, battlesites, and blockades

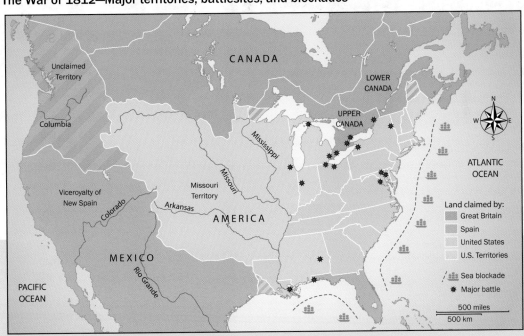

BIBLIOGRAPHY

QUOTATIONS

p. 4 Historical Narratives of Early Canada: http://www.uppercanadahistory.ca/brock/brock4.html
p. 8 *An Essay by David Thelen: History Making in America.* http://onlinelibrary.wiley.com/doi/10.1111/j.1540-6563.1991.tb00825.x/abstract
p. 16 Cicero quote from http://www.azquotes.com/author/2894-Marcus_Tullius_Cicero/tag/history
p. 20 James Madison, letter of January 5, 1804. www.loc.gov/resource/mjm.08_0698_0703/?st=gallery
p. 34 D. Peter MacLeod. *Four Wars of 1812.* Madeira Park, British Columbia: Douglas & McIntyre, 2012.
p. 38 Kevin Gover quote. https://www.npr.org/sections/codeswitch/2015/01/18/368559990/broken-promises-on-display-at-native-american-treaties-exhibit

EXCERPTS

p.7 From the U.S. Declaration of Independence, signed on July 4, 1776.
p. 11 Robert Livingston, quoted in "America's Louisiana Purchase: Noble Bargain, Difficult Journey." http://www.lpb.org/index.php?/site/programs/americas_louisiana_purchase
p. 12 Felix Grundy quote: http://www.ucl.ac.uk/USHistory/Building/docs/1812.htm
p. 14 Harrison quote: http://novelzec.com/chapter/four_american_indians/chapter_14
p. 19 John Adams quote from *Argument in Defense of the Soldiers in the Boston Massacre Trial*, December 1770 from http://www.quotationspage.com/quote/3235.html
p. 25 *The Voice of Warning!*, New York, 1810. http://collections.libraries.indiana.edu/warof1812/exhibits/show/warof1812/before/war-hawks
p. 27 American Captain Joseph Hopper Nicholson, May 20, 1814. https://maryland1812.wordpress.com/2011/03/12/baltimore-quotes-of-war1814/
p. 28 Thomas Jefferson, 1812, quoted in Williams, Gomer. *History of the Liverpool Privateers and Letters of Marque.* New York: Augustus M. Kelley, 1897.
p. 31 Stanley Clisby Arthur, quoted in *Louisiana Historical Society*, September 25, 2017.
p. 32 The Duke of Wellington, 1814, quoted in Mills, D. "The Duke of Wellington and the peace negotiations at Ghent in 1814." *Canadian Historical Review.* 2 (1), 1921, p. 22.

p. 37 Tecumseh, 1812, quoted in Clarke, Peter Dooyentate. *Origins and Traditional History of the Wyandotts and Sketches of Other Indian Tribes of North America: True Traditional Stories of Tecumseh and his league, in the years 1811 and 1812.* Toronto, Canada: Hunter, Rose & Co, 1870. p. 93.
p. 40. Tecumseh's speech to Governor William Harrison, August 11, 1810. http://images.indianahistory.org/cdm/ref/collection/dc007/id/19f

TO FIND OUT MORE

Alvarez, Pilar F. *The War of 1812: New Challenges for a New Nation.* PowerKids Press, 2017.

Clarke, Gordon; Flatt, Lizann; Isaacs, Sally Senzell; Johnson, Robin. Various titles in *War of 1812* series. Crabtree Publishing, 2012.

Fulton, Kristen and Holly Berry. *Long May She Wave: The True Story of Caroline Pickersgill and Her Star-Spangled Creation.* Margaret K. McElderry Books, 2017.

O'Neill, Robert and Carl Benn. *The War of 1812: The Fight for American Trade Rights.* Rosen Publishing, 2011.

Zimmerman, Dwight Jon. *Tecumseh: Shooting Star of the Shawnee.* Sterling, 2010.

INTERNET GUIDELINES

Finding good source material on the Internet can sometimes be a challenge. When analyzing how reliable the information is, consider these points:

- Who is the author of the page? Is it an expert in the field or a person who experienced the event?
- Is the site well known and up to date? A page that has not been updated for several years probably has out-of-date information.
- Can you verify the facts with another site? Always double-check information.

- Have you checked all possible sites? Don't just look on the first page a search engine provides. Remember to try government sites and research papers.
- Have you recorded website addresses and names? Keep this data so you can backtrack and verify the information you want to use.

WEBSITES:

The War of 1812
Articles and videos about James Madison and the history of the war.
http://www.history.com/topics/war-of-1812

Resources relating to the War of 1812
Lesson plans, details of an exhibition about the war, and aids to research—from the government of Ontario, Canada.
http://www.archives.gov.on.ca/en/1812/index.aspx

Naval Battles
Learn all about the naval battles of the war from U.S. Naval History and Heritage Command.
https://www.history.navy.mil

Military Heritage
An overview of the war from an independent Canadian historical organization.
http://warof1812.ca/

Niagara Parks
Heritage center with artifacts and memorials related to the war.
https://www.niagaraparks.com/visit-niagara-parks/heritage/plaques-markers/

Library of Congress
A selection of images related to the war, from the U.S. archive.
https://www.loc.gov/rr/print/list/war_1812.html

The U.S.S. *Chesapeake*
Information about one of the most important ships of the war.
http://www.theusschesapeake.com/

GLOSSARY

accurate Correct in all details

allies Nations that are on the same side in a war

amendment A change or addition made to a proposal or document

American Revolutionary War A conflict in North America between Great Britain and its 13 colonies on the East Coast, which were fighting for independence. Also known as the War of Independence, it lasted from 1775 to 1783.

analyzed Examined closely

archive A place that stores historical information about a location, a person, or an event

artifacts Objects made by human beings

bias Prejudice in favor of or against one thing, person, or group compared with another

blockading Isolating or cutting off enemy positions or ports by troops or ships in order to prevent the passage of troops and supplies

buffer territory An area located between two powerful, and possibly rival, countries

broadside A sheet of newspaper printed on one side only designed to be made widely available

citizens People who have full rights to live in a country

colony An area that belongs to and is governed by a faraway country. Great Britain, France, and Spain each had colonies in North America.

Columbia The young woman representing the United States of America

confederacy A group of people who come together for a specific purpose such as to negotiate a treaty

Congress In the United States, two groups of representatives who make laws for the nation—the Senate and the House of Representatives

context The setting in which an event occurs

credible Something that can be believed

culture The arts, traditions, and other achievements of a certain society

democracy A political system in which government is made up of representatives elected by all adult citizens

economy Creating, earning, and spending wealth

enslaved peoples People who are owned by another person, do not have any rights, and are treated as property

evidence Information or objects related to an event

expansionism A policy of territorial or economic expansion or growth

exports Goods and services sold abroad

fleet A group of ships that travels together, often for protection

free trade Trade between nations without interference such as taxes

frigate A small, fast, naval ship used for patrol and escort duties

impress To force people to serve as sailors or soldiers

independence Being separate from another country and having one's own government

Indigenous peoples The original inhabitants of a country

infantry Troops who fight on foot

John Bull The plump, middle-age man representing Great Britain, especially England. He is the equivalent of the U.S. Uncle Sam.

legacy What one inherits or receives from an event

militia A small army of citizens organized by each state who serve as solders in emergencies

Napoleonic Wars Wars in Europe from 1803 to 1815 between the French Empire led by Napoléon Bonaparte and other countries including Great Britain

neutral Not supporting or helping either side in a war

Northwest Territory Land in the United States that was being settled in the 1790s; it included present-day Ohio, Indiana, Illinois, Michigan, Wisconsin, and parts of Minnesota

perspectives Points of view or ways of looking at something

piracy The practice of attacking and robbing ships at sea

primary sources Firsthand accounts or direct evidence of an event

privateering Outfitting a privately owned merchant ship for war

protested People showing their strong feelings against something or someone

province An administrative division, or region of a country

rampart A defensive or protective barrier

ratified Gave formal assent to a treaty

regular Full-time; "regulars" are career soldiers or sailors

republic A country in which supreme power is held by the people and their elected representatives

reservations Areas of land set aside by governments for Indigenous peoples to live on

revolution The forcible overthrow of a government or a social order in a favor of a new system

secondary sources Materials created by studying primary sources

Senate One of two parts of the U.S. government that makes the laws; part of Congress, along with the House of Representatives

Six Nations The six Iroquois tribes: Mohawk, Cayuga, Onondaga, Oneida, Seneca, and Tuscarora

source materials Original documents or other pieces of evidence

territory A region belonging to or governed by a state or country

treaties Formal agreements between two or more parties, usually to prevent or end wars

tyrant A leader who is oppressive and harsh, maintaining their power by any means necessary

INDEX